THIS BOOK BELONGS TO:

....

Al-Aqsa Publishers
P.O. Box 5127
Leicester
LE2 0WU

E-mail: info@aqsa.org.uk | Website: www.aqsa.org.uk

Illustrated by Ghazala Caratella

Design and Layout by Shoayb Adam

With special thanks to Sanam Mirza

The Prophets in Palestine

Prophet Yusuf عليه السلام

Prophet Yusuf عليه السلام was a very handsome man. In fact, he was given half of the world's beauty by Allah سبحانه وتعالى, and he had a face that shone like the moon.

But this wasn't the only blessing that Allah سبحانه وتعالى granted him.

Yusuf عليه السلام came from a long line of prophets – beginning with the Prophet Ibrahim عليه السلام, who was his great grandfather. His grandfather was Prophet Ishaq عليه السلام and his father was Prophet Yaqub عليه السلام.

All of his forefathers were prophets of Allah سبحانه وتعالى because Prophet Ibrahim عليه السلام made du'a asking for his family to be blessed with guidance.

When Yusuf ﷵ was a young boy he had a dream. He saw eleven stars, the sun and the moon bow down to him.

Yusuf ﷵ told his father about this strange dream. His father told him to be careful and not to tell anyone else about it. He knew that there was something very special about his son and that Allah ﷻ would give him the power to interpret dreams, and make him a very important person.

Yusuf ﷺ had eleven brothers and the youngest was called Binyamin (Benjamin). They all lived near Jerusalem in Palestine, which at that time was called Canaan.

Prophet Yaqub ﷺ loved all of his twelve sons. However, Yusuf's ﷺ brothers felt jealous, apart from Binyamin, because they thought that their father loved Yusuf ﷺ more than them.

The brothers were so jealous of Yusuf ﷵ that they decided to do a terrible thing. They wanted to get rid of Yusuf ﷵ forever.

They decided to come up with a plan.

One of them suggested that they should kill Yusuf ﷵ! Others thought it would be better if they sent him to a faraway place. Finally, they decided to take him away from their home, and throw him into a well.

One day, when Yusuf's ﷵ brothers had decided on their evil plan, they told their father that they wanted to take Yusuf ﷵ out with them to play. Yusuf’s ﷵ father was unsure because he knew that they were jealous of him. His brothers kept asking and said that they would take good care of him.

But they were lying; really they had another plan.

Finally, their father said yes, and warned them to be careful.

The brothers set off, and when they were a long way away from their home, they did what they had planned. They threw Yusuf ﵇ into a well!

Allah ﷾ knew everything that was happening. He told Yusuf ﵇ not to worry and that He ﷾ would take care of Yusuf ﵇.

When the brothers returned home to their father without Yusuf ﵇, they acted out a careful plan to convince their father that Yusuf ﵇ had been eaten by wild animals. They even brought a shirt stained with the blood of an animal to prove to their father that Yusuf ﵇ was dead. The reaction of their father in that difficult moment was amazing.

The brothers pretended to cry and look upset. Their father knew that this was a lie, but still, he didn't get upset at them, even though he had warned them to be careful.

Instead, he told them that he would be patient and trust Allah ﷻ. He knew that Allah ﷻ would never let him down.

Meanwhile Yusuf عليه السلام was still in the well. A group of travellers on their way to Egypt found him when they stopped for water. This was a blessing from Allah سبحانه وتعالى because it meant that he could come out from the well. The travellers were happy to find him. They took him from Palestine and sold him as a slave in Egypt.

Yusuf عليه السلام had gone from being free to being sold as a slave and this was a test from Allah سبحانه وتعالى. But Allah سبحانه وتعالى was still there to help him.

In the end, Yusuf عليه السلام was bought as a slave by the governor of Egypt!

As Yusuf عليه السلام grew up into a young man, his beauty also increased and many people found him very attractive. The wife of the governor was one of these people. But Yusuf عليه السلام was an honest man and didn't like all the attention.

Women in Egypt started gossiping that the wife of the governor liked Yusuf عليه السلام. The women in the city started to look down on the wife of the governor for liking her slave.

To teach them a lesson, the wife of the governor invited the women to a banquet and gave them each a knife to cut their fruit with. While the women were cutting the fruit, the wife of the governor called Yusuf عليه السلام. When the women saw him, they were so shocked by how beautiful he was that they accidentally cut their fingers!

The wife of the governor wanted to show them so that they didn't blame her for liking him.

Finally, the wife of the governor decided to try to make Yusuf عليه السلام like her. She was alone in a room with Yusuf عليه السلام, and she locked the door and tried to hug him.

Yusuf عليه السلام prayed to Allah سبحانه وتعالى to protect him and ran away from her. As he was running away, the governor came into the room. The governor's wife knew that she would be in trouble so she lied to her husband and said that Yusuf عليه السلام had tried to attack her!

Yusuf عليه السلام was innocent but because the wife had a high position in Egypt, he was put in prison. This was another great test from Allah سبحانه وتعالى.

When he was in prison, Yusuf عليه السلام met two other men. They saw that he was a very special person and asked for his advice about a dream they had each had. They wanted to know what their dreams meant, and Yusuf عليه السلام could explain dreams.

Before Yusuf explained their dream, he wanted to call them to Allah سبحانه وتعالى and so gave them da’wah.

Both men described their dreams.

Yusuf عليه السلام told one of the men that his dream meant that he was going to be killed.

He told the other man he was going to be freed and would press wine for the king of Egypt.

Yusuf عليه السلام then asked this man to tell the king about him when he was freed.

Some time later, the man was freed, just as Yusuf عليه السلام had said he would be. However, Shaytaan made the man forget his promise to Yusuf عليه السلام and so he didn't tell the king about him.

One day the king of Egypt had a troubling dream that nobody could explain. The king dreamt that seven fat cows were eaten by seven thin cows. He also saw seven healthy ears of corn and seven others that were dried up.

Just then, the man who had been freed from prison remembered Yusuf عليه السلام, because he knew that Yusuf عليه السلام could explain what dreams meant. He asked the king if he could go and see Yusuf عليه السلام in prison.

Yusuf ﷺ interpreted the dream and he gave some advice about the difficult times that were coming for the people in Egypt.

Yusuf ﷺ explained that the dream meant that for the next seven years, there would be a lot of food but in the seven years after that, there will be very little food because of bad weather. He advised them to save plenty of food in the first seven years, or people would be very poor and hungry.

34

When the king heard this, he wanted to see Yusuf عليه السلام.

Yusuf عليه السلام was told that he was free to leave the prison, but his response was very surprising!

Instead of rushing to leave prison where he had spent such a long time, Yusuf عليه السلام decided that he would not leave until people knew that the wife of the governor had lied about him. He wanted to prove that he was innocent.

The king demanded that the woman who had lied about Yusuf عليه السلام come to him, and asked what had happened. She admitted that Yusuf عليه السلام was innocent and pure.

Having cleared his name, Yusuf عليه السلام left the prison a free man and everybody knew that he was innocent.

The king was very impressed and wanted Yusuf عليه السلام to work for him. Yusuf عليه السلام asked if he could be put in charge of the food store houses in Egypt because he knew that there would be a famine years later. Allah سبحانه وتعالى had blessed him with knowledge and wisdom and he was the best person for this job.

When the famine came, it affected everybody in the area, and the family of Yusuf ﵇ in Palestine also suffered. This made the brothers of Yusuf ﵇ leave their home and travel to Egypt to find food for their family.

When they arrived, Yusuf ﵇ immediately recognised his brothers but saw that his youngest brother Binyamin was missing. He asked if they had left one of their brothers behind with their father. Yusuf ﵇ gave them a bag of food each and told them to return with the younger brother, and he would then give them more food.

The brothers were very excited and told their father to let Binyamin travel with them to Egypt. They promised to bring him back safely with them, just as they did years ago with Yusuf عليه السلام. Their father had not forgotten this, but after some time, he agreed.

When the brothers of Yusuf عليه السلام went back to Egypt with Binyamin, Yusuf عليه السلام had made a plan. He spoke to Binyamin alone, and told him who he was.

Yusuf عليه السلام then gave all of his brothers more bags of food but also placed one of the king's precious cups in Binyamin's bag.

When the guards found that the cup was missing, they ordered that all the bags were checked.

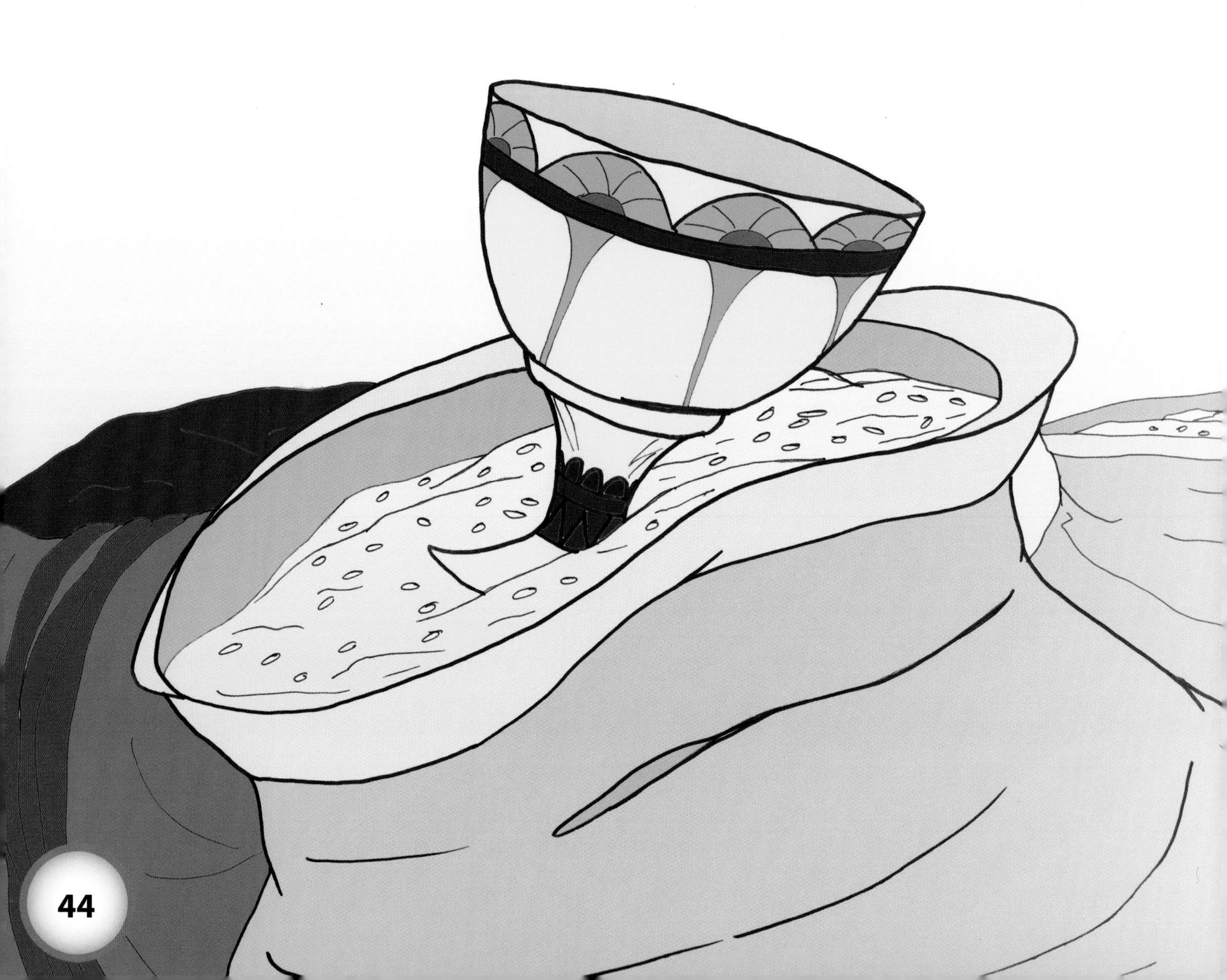

The brothers were asked what should happen to the person who had stolen the cup. They agreed that the thief should have to stay behind and be a slave in Egypt.

Yusuf عليه السلام then pulled the cup out from Binyamin's bag, knowing that Binyamin would now be able to stay with him.

The brothers of Yusuf عليه السلام were upset that the king's cup was with Binyamin, and remembered the promise they had made in Allah's name to their father that they would bring Binyamin back safely. They pleaded with Yusuf عليه السلام to let Binyamin leave with them, but Yusuf عليه السلام refused.

When the brothers realised that they would have to go back home without Binyamin, just as they had done with Yusuf عليه السلام years ago, they argued over what they should tell their father.

They made the journey back to their home and told their father Yaqub عليه السلام exactly what had happened. But Yaqub عليه السلام didn't believe that Binyamin would steal. He knew that Binyamin had a good character and he wasn't a thief.

Yaqub عليه السلام gave his sons the same reply that he had given them so many years earlier – that it would be best to be patient, and he prayed that Allah سبحانه وتعالى return his children to him.

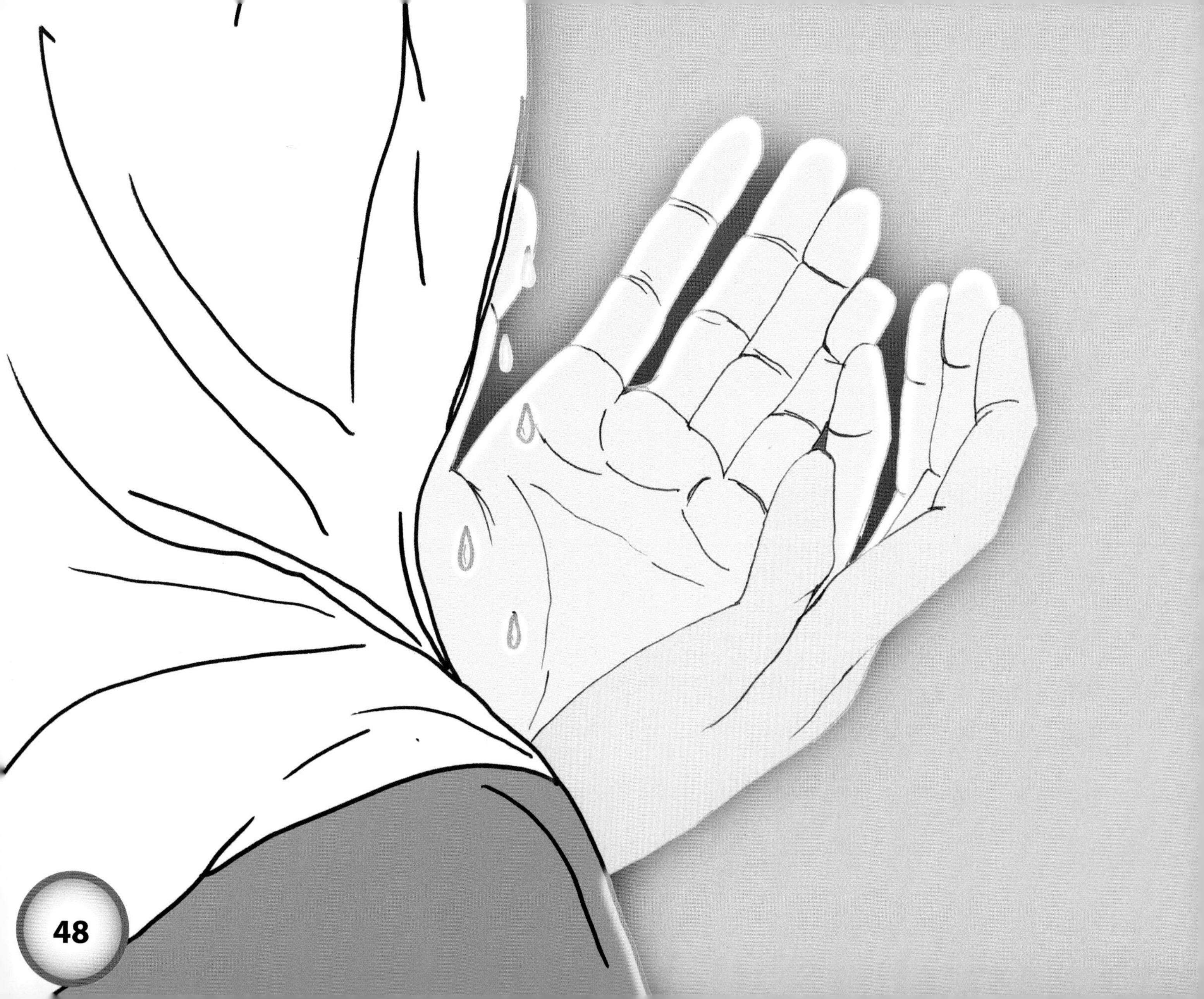

Even though Yaqub ﷺ had complete trust in Allah ﷻ, he was very sad at the loss of his two sons and he cried to Allah ﷻ a great deal. After some time, because of his sadness, he became blind.

When the time came for the brothers to return to Egypt for more food, Yaqub ﷺ told his sons to try to find Yusuf ﷺ and Binyamin.

On this third trip to Egypt the brothers of Yusuf عليه السلام were very, very poor. They only had a few things to trade and so begged Yusuf عليه السلام to have mercy on them.

Now Yusuf عليه السلام was in a better position than his brothers! When he was little, the brothers of Yusuf عليه السلام had been cruel and unkind to him and because of that, Yusuf عليه السلام had to go through a lot of difficulty. But now it was them who needed his help.

When he saw the desperate state they were in, he thought to ask them one simple question.

"Do you now realise what you did to Yusuf?"

Stunned by the question, the brothers of Yusuf عليه السلام realised that it was only their brother Yusuf عليه السلام who knew what happened and could have asked them this.

Years after they had left him alone in the well, the brothers now saw Yusuf عليه السلام in an honoured position, much higher than them. They realised that they had done wrong.

Then came the most amazing part.

Even though Yusuf عليه السلام had been through so much because of what his brothers had done to him, he didn't get upset at them. In fact, he told them that they weren't going to be blamed for what they did, and he made dua for them.

This shows that no matter how badly people can sometimes treat us, we must fill our hearts with love and forgiveness.

Yusuf عليه السلام asked his brothers to do two things.

First, he asked them to take his shirt and lay it over their father's face.

Second, he asked them to bring the whole family to Egypt.

The brothers listened, and when they went back and placed the shirt over their father's face, a miracle occurred. He was able to see again!

The brothers were feeling terrible about what they had made their father go through. They turned to him with sadness. But their father Yaqub عليه السلام did not get upset at his sons, but prayed to Allah سبحانه وتعالى for His forgiveness.

Now that he was cured, Yaqub عليه السلام, his sons and their families travelled from Palestine to Egypt. When they reached Egypt and found Yusuf عليه السلام, they were delighted and bowed down to him out of respect.

This was the dream Yusuf عليه السلام had as a child that had come true. The parents of Yusuf عليه السلام were the sun and moon in his dream, and his brothers were the stars.

This did not make Yusuf عليه السلام proud, but he was humbled by the mercy that Allah سبحانه وتعالى showed to him. Yusuf عليه السلام prayed to Allah سبحانه وتعالى to make him a steadfast and righteous slave for the rest of his life.

There are so many lessons in the story of Yusuf عليه السلام. We see how Yusuf عليه السلام was patient, honest and trustworthy in good times and bad. We see how he forgave his brothers even though they treated him cruelly. And we see that even though he was forgiving and loving, that didn't stop him from standing up for himself when the wife of the governor lied about him.

The Prophet Yusuf ﷺ is an inspiration to so many people and we can learn so much from his story.

What did you learn from his story?